JANET WILSON MEETS THE QUEEN

Janet Wilson Meets the Queen

Beverley Cooper

Janet Wilson Meets the Queen
first published 2018 by Scirocco Drama
An imprint of J. Gordon Shillingford Publishing Inc.

Scirocco Drama Editor: Glenda MacFarlane
Cover design by Terry Gallagher/Doowah Design
Author photo by Corrine Koslo

Printed and bound in Canada on 100% post-consumer recycled paper.
We acknowledge the financial support of the Manitoba Arts Council and
The Canada Council for the Arts for our publishing program.

For production rights contact:
Suzanne DePoe
CTI Artist Management
483 Euclid Ave.
Toronto, Ontario.
M6G 2T1
416-944-0475
suzanne@ctiam.ca

Library and Archives Canada Cataloguing in Publication

Cooper, Beverley, author
Janet Wilson meets the Queen / Beverley Cooper. -- First edition.

A play.
ISBN 978-1-927922-44-6 (softcover)

I. Title.

PS8555.O5884J36 2018 C812'.54 C2018-904636-8

J. Gordon Shillingford Publishing
P.O. Box 86, RPO Corydon Avenue, Winnipeg, MB Canada R3M 3S3

To the man I love, one of the good ones, John Jarvis

Beverley Cooper

Beverley Cooper is a writer, actor, and teacher. She has written for TV, film, and extensively for CBC radio drama, twice being nominated for Writers' Guild of Canada Awards. Her plays have been produced across Canada, including *Clue in the Fast Lane* (co-written with Ann-Marie MacDonald); *Thin Ice* (co-written with Banuta Rubess, Chalmers / Dora Award); *The Eyes of Heaven*; *The Woman in White* (adapted from the novel by Wilkie Collins); *The Lonely Diner: Al Capone in Euphemia Township; Janet Wilson Meets the Queen* (nominated for Prix Rideau Award) and, most recently, *If Truth Be Told. Innocence Lost: A Play about Steven Truscott* was a finalist for a Governor General's Literary Award and was on the *Globe and Mail* Bestsellers List, a first for a Canadian playwright.

Beverley trained as an actor and has performed in TV, film and in theatres across Canada. She holds an MFA in Creative Writing from the University of Guelph and has presented her work at WPI conferences in India, Stockholm, and Cape Town. She recently began directing audio books for Penguin Random House.

Beverley is the coordinator of The CASA Project, a charitable arm of the Playwrights Guild of Canada Women's Caucus, which aims to support women playwrights living in South Africa.

For more information about Beverley's work, visit: www.BeverleyCooper.com

Playwright's Notes

Janet Wilson Meets the Queen arose from a desire to write a play about political apathy. Why is it so difficult for us to look at what is going on in the world? Why are some people engaged in politics, trying to change things for the better, fighting for social justice…while others are unable to? *Janet Wilson Meets the Queen* is set during the years 1969 through 1971, a time of huge political and social upheaval: women's rights, Black rights, the Vietnam war, rise of the FLQ… The world was changing quickly and drastically. It was also the time of my own political awakening and the beginning of my personal battle against an inclination to stare at something bright and shiny, rather than looking at the dark and difficult side of life. I am very fond of Janet Wilson and hope she will make you laugh, reflect, and engage.

I began writing *Janet Wilson* while I was getting my MFA in Creative Writing at the University of Guelph. I was in a class led by the remarkable playwright Judith Thompson, who poked and prodded me to let the writing flow. The writing continued under a mentorship with the esteemed Smith College teacher Len Berkman. I still treasure his enthusiastic, insightful and encouraging emails. The (late) dramaturge extraordinaire Iris Turcott dissected subsequent drafts and provoked me into writing a much better play. Many thanks goes to those three individuals, as well as my fellow MFA-ers (particularly Robert Chafe, Eufemia Fantetti and Naoko Kumagai); Diana Belshaw and the acting students at Humber College; Nina Lee Aquino and Factory Theatre, who hosted a workshop with actors Sarah Dodd, Vivien Endicott-Douglas, Patricia Hamilton, and Noah Reid. Financial support happily arrived from the Ontario Arts Council and via The Canadian Federation of University Women's Dr. Alice E. Wilson Award. And finally, thank you

Eric, Andrea, and the remarkable GCTC team who threw their hearts and souls into the first, shining production.

We would rather be ruined than changed;
We would rather die in our dread
Than climb the cross of the moment
And let our illusions die.

– W.H. Auden

Production History

Janet Wilson Meets the Queen was first produced by The Great Canadian Theatre Company in Ottawa, Ontario, under the expert guidance of Artistic Director Eric Coates. Opening day April 21st, 2016 (on the occasion of the Queen's 90th birthday), with the following creative team:

Janet Wilson .... Marion Day
Granny .... Beverley Wolfe
Lily .... Katie Ryerson
Robbie / Moonwalker / Jim .... Tony Adams

Director: Andrea Donaldson
Set and Costume Design: Roger Schultz
Lighting Design: Martin Conboy
Sound Design: Thomas Ryder Payne
Stage Manager: Laurie Champagne
Assistant Stage Manager: Jess Preece

Characters

JANET 40s

Lilibet (LILY) .... 15–17, her daughter

GRANNY .... 70s, Janet's mother

ROBBIE .... 19–21, cousin from San Francisco

MOONWALKER

JIM .... Janet's husband

The actor who plays ROBBIE can double as MOONWALKER and JIM. The actor playing LILY can play the MOONWALKER in Act One, Scene 9.

Setting

Act One: Vancouver, Canada. 1969

Act Two: Vancouver, Canada. 1971

The set is more suggestive than realistic, so that several playing areas can be active without big scene changes.

Act One

1. Doing the Impossible

We hear: the crackly soundtrack of Neil Armstrong walking on the moon, eventually mixing with music, music with a bit of magic in it: Moon Music. We see: MOONWALKER, a man in a space suit, walking on the moon, as close as possible to the images we have seen on TV: striding and floating. An American flag is planted firmly in the moon's soil.

2. Everything Is All Right With the World or Is It?

The Fall, Vancouver, 1969.

The Moon Music continues. Light up on JANET. She wears a housedress over a nice dress.

JANET: This summer a man walked on the moon. Isn't that just the most remarkable thing? The Apollo 11 took Neil Armstrong all the way to that faraway orb so he could take his historic steps on behalf of all of mankind: floating, bouncing – so effortlessly – on our moon. And guess who was there, right along with him, giving Mr. Armstrong strength and guidance. Her Majesty, Queen Elizabeth the Second, by the Grace of God, of Great Britain, Ireland and the British Dominions beyond the Seas, Defender of the Faith.

Of course, I don't mean Our Queen was actually on the moon. *(Small chuckle.)* I am sure, just like all of us, she was transfixed in front of her television set…probably at Balmoral for the summer holidays; Prince Philip sitting comfortably on the sofa; two or three freshly washed and combed corgis sleeping on the Royal Aster carpet that was a gift from the Turkish ambassador in 1902; their well-behaved children watching earnestly; Princess Anne, fresh from a ride on her horse, Peebles; Prince Charles, his young shoulders preparing to take on his life's purpose...

GRANNY: *(Offstage.)* That Charles looks like an old boot. He's got sticky-outy ears.

JANET: No, rather Our Beloved Queen sent a *personal message* with the Apollo mission, a message that was microfilmed, sealed in a time capsule and then left on the moon, placed in the perfectly named…Sea of Tranquility. Her message being: "I salute the skill and courage which have brought man to the moon. May this endeavour increase the knowledge and well-being of mankind."

And with her moon-bound message, Queen Elizabeth not only gives us hope for the future, but also sends along our past as well: her great regal ancestry: Queen Victoria, Mary Queen of Scotts, Henry the Eighth. House of Windsor, Hanover, Tudor…Our Queen is the human embodiment of all that history! And Charles, the newly anointed Prince of Wales will carry on that lineage with –

GRANNY: *(Offstage.)* He's horsey-looking, he looks like Mr. Ed!

Light up on GRANNY. The magic music fades.

JANET: Charles may not be handsome in a Rock Hudson sense but when you have those ancient genes, each of those kings and queens struggling to come to the surface of your face, battling to claim the mark of their ancestry, it's very difficult –

GRANNY: What's the use of a queen in the first place, complete waste of taxpayers' money. Why do we want to tie ourselves to Great Britain anyway? They're all so snooty.

JANET: For Pete's sake, Mother, don't bring that up tonight or I'll never hear the end of it.

GRANNY: We should just become part of the United States. What's the difference? They've got better TV, cheaper clothes, and I like those Bounty chocolate bars.

JANET sighs and takes some recipe cards out to check her notes.

JANET: Shoot. I got it wrong again, it's Stuarts, then Tudors... Oh dear...can that be? I had better check on that. I don't want Sheila Witherspoon down my neck. *(Calling offstage.)* Jim, can you pull out the "T" from the Funk and Wagnalls?...

Lights up on JIM, he's sitting in an armchair in a corner watching sports on TV, with Howard Cosell commentating. He has a TV table at his side.

What do you think, so far, Jim?....Have you been listening?....

GRANNY: What'll they be serving for dinner?

JANET tries to get her recipe cards in the right order.

JANET: I believe there's a buffet after the ceremonies.

GRANNY: I hate buffets. It's like pigs at a trough. Pigs with sharp, pointy elbows.

JANET: Then I'll get you a plate and bring it to the table.

GRANNY: I don't want to go.

JANET: The Lieutenant Governor is coming so there should be a good crowd… Don't you want to hear my speech, Mum? It's quite an honour to be asked, you know.

GRANNY: I've just heard it.

JANET: Well, I'm not making you supper. Not when I've already bought you a ticket for the dinner.

GRANNY: Get in front of the line so you get the beef that's cooked. Gravy on the potatoes. Green beans and carrots. No peas. I don't like mushy peas.

JANET: All right, Mother, I need to practise my speech, there's only – For Pete's sake, look at the time. Jim! We have to leave shortly! Have you still got your work clothes on?

GRANNY: Remember when Amy was chosen to present flowers to Dean Martin? He was singing the "O Canada" somewhere or other. I sewed her a yellow hairband to match the yellow daffodils. She looked absolutely lovely. What a day that was. Dean Martin said she was as sweet as butterscotch taffy.

JANET reads from her notes.

JANET: "Queen Elizabeth is our greatest example of devotion to service, constantly reminding us, simply by her presence, that there is a higher cause, principles more important than our own petty desires – "

GRANNY: Get to the point a little quicker.

JANET: Mother, please –

GRANNY: What is the point, anyway?

JANET: The point is always the same point and you know it. The point is our absolute support for the British monarchy. The point is this is the first time I have been asked to give the speech to the Imperial Order Daughters of the Empire Fundraising Dinner since I joined fifteen years ago! Sheila Witherspoon has done it umpteen times!

JANET takes a chocolate bar out of her pocket, then thinks better of it and puts it back.

GRANNY: I want horseradish with the roast beef.

JANET: It might be casseroles.

GRANNY: Lord love a duck, why bother then?!

Sound of a record being played, something light and poppy – suggested style: "Dizzy" by Tommy Roe. It starts soft and then gradually gets louder.

You need to keep that girl in tow. She's been wearing makeup again.

She looks like a prostitute.

JANET: Mother! She's only fifteen, she hardly looks like a –

GRANNY: You didn't wear makeup until your wedding day.

JANET: Please don't tell me how to raise my daughter –

GRANNY: I won't say a word. Even if she's doing the Watusi in front of a steamroller, I won't say a word.

JANET: Lily! Almost time to go!

The music and TV are gradually getting louder as JANET tries gamely to keep talking. A TV ad plays: "Ring around the collar, Ring around the collar!!" JANET reads from her notes.

"And as Elizabeth guided those astronauts: doing what no one thought ever possible, walking on the moon, thousands of miles away, a magical place of storybooks,/ glowing amongst the stars, lit only by the flaming sun, so she guides us all, through the difficulties of our daily lives, reminding us that – "

GRANNY: *(Overlapping previous line.)* /Your slip is showing at the back, a full three inches… And did you know your stocking has a run?

JANET: COULD I PLEASE HAVE SOME PEACE AND QUIET FOR TWO MINUTES???? IS THAT TOO MUCH TO ASK???

The volume of the music and TV lowers as Janet tries to pull herself together, ignore her mother and go through her notes as:

GRANNY: Listen, Miss Hoity-Toity Queen Lover, I don't want to be living here any more than you want me living with you. It wasn't my choice.

You tricked me, like a spider with a fly. I had one bad day and you pounced. All I wanted was some Niblets and a bit of liver to make my dinner. That's all I was doing. I didn't know the price of Niblets had gone up. It's that Woodwards chickie's fault. Huffing and puffing, snapping her gum, getting me all flustered. And Chickie has the cheek to ask if I want her to count the coins. Takes my coin purse and dumps it out on the thingy… I was only fifteen cents short. "What do you want to do? " she says… I tell you what I want to do. I want to go back in time when I had a thick pile of bills in my leather wallet. I want to not have to take umpteen horse pills a day for high blood pressure, arrhythmia and that G.D. pain in my joints. I want to go to more weddings and baby showers than funerals. I want to remember dates and places and who said what. I want to pick up the Niblets and whack that smirk off her stupid face! The idiot panics and calls you.

JANET: Lily! Can you come here?

GRANNY: I know you don't want me living with you.

Pause.

I miss my house, my things…my Brown Betty and my china cabinet… I miss my pink peonies, the smell of the lilacs. I miss my kitchen! I want to cook my own food. Date meringues, toad-in-a-hole, lamb chops with mint jelly, meatloaf with tomato sauce, roast beef and Yorkshire puddings –

JANET: Right now, Lily!

GRANNY: Just you wait until you begin the final, slow, godawful slide towards the end of life. I can tell you… It ain't any bowl of peaches.

JANET calmly puts the recipe cards back in her pocket.

JANET: Mother. Do you need use the little girls' room before we go? Don't want any accidents tonight.

GRANNY: Lord love a duck.

LILY enters. She wears a Ranger uniform.

JANET: Hope you've been practising, we've only got a few minutes before push-off time.

LILY: I don't want to sing in front of everyone.

GRANNY: Look at her eyes. You see?

JANET: You're just nervous. When I was your age, I entered an oratory contest and I didn't sleep for two weeks, I was so anxious.

LILY: Yeah?

GRANNY: Her lids are slathered in it.

JANET: I had to speak about the Peoples of Mesopotamia. Turned out to be a real barnburner. I got a shiny blue ribbon. And in the end I was very glad I did it.

LILY: All right. But don't expect *me* to be any good.

JANET: Your scarf isn't done up properly.

JANET redoes LILY's scarf. Low, to LILY so GRANNY doesn't hear:

Now wash that makeup off your face, this isn't a masquerade party.

LILY leaves. JANET takes off her housedress and is able to roll up her slip as:

GRANNY: I don't remember any oratory contest.

JANET: Jiiiim! Get changed! Your Sunday pants are ironed and on the bed.

JANET remembers the comment about the run in the stocking and looks at it, dismayed. She gets some clear nail polish out of her purse and applies it on the run as:

LILY: *(Offstage, she starts to sing an approximated version of* The Lord's Prayer. *As she goes along she bops it up a bit.)* Our Father, Who art in Heaven, hallowèd be thy name, thy Kingdom Come, thy will be done, hallowèd be thy name…

As JANET listens, she slyly takes a chocolate bar out of her pocket, and nibbles a piece, like it's Valium.

JANET: Jim! Did you hear me? It's time to go!!

3. This Is Not the Family I Wanted

JANET has on a nice apron. She is serving a plate of food to GRANNY. JIM is watching TV.

JANET: Jim, Lily, dinnertime!

GRANNY: What's that?

JANET: It's called Shake 'n Bake. Doesn't it look tasty?

GRANNY: Never heard of it.

JANET: You put the chicken in a bag with the coating, shake it and bake it. I hope you will keep an open mind, Mum.

GRANNY: Don't worry about me, I can just pick it off.

JANET: Mother. Please.

GRANNY: At least it's hot, more than I can say for that inedible dinner last night. Kidney pie! What were those people thinking?

JANET: I won't have you ruin my memory of a lovely night.

GRANNY: I hope you always remember Jim snoring like an ape during your speech.

JANET: If you can't say anything nice, please don't say anything at all.

GRANNY: Or Missy there forgetting her words to the Lord's Prayer. Hope you remember that.

JANET: *I'm* still floating on a cloud from that announcement.

GRANNY: Which announcement?

JANET: That in two years it will be British Columbia's centennial of joining Canada. *(Pause.)* Of course, it's easy to put two and two together, that if the Queen came to Montreal for Expo, it's very likely she'll come *here* for a royal tour, too. Wouldn't that be a thrill?

GRANNY: I'm not saying anything at all.

LILY comes in wearing a skirt she's rolled up to be very short.

JANET: Lily! What happened to your skirt?

LILY: What?

JANET: So much leg is showing.

LILY: Don't be square, Mum.

JANET: You've rolled it up? What on earth?

LILY: Everybody is wearing their skirts short now.

JANET: I don't think so. Unroll it, please.

LILY: Oh, brother.

JANET places dinner in front of LILY.

What's this?

JANET: It's the Shake 'n Bake you asked me to buy.

LILY: It looks like someone barfed on the chicken.

JANET: Lily!

LILY: Don't get mad at me. I didn't know it was going to look like this.

JANET: I'm not getting mad at you. Please say grace… Jim, we're starting without you!

LILY: For what we are about to receive may the Lord make us truly grateful, Amen.

GRANNY and JANET start eating.

Dibs on the TV at eight. *Brady Bunch* is on.

GRANNY: Age before beauty. I'm watching *Let's Make a Deal.*

LILY: Are you joking? I've been living here longer than you.

GRANNY: I'd like to take you over my knee and whack your bee-hind until it's swollen like a pumpkin.

JANET: Enough!! There will be no TV watching unless a certain someone gets her homework done.

LILY: I don't need to do homework. I'm going to be a dancer.

JANET: You are? You haven't taken any lessons.

LILY: You don't need to have lessons to be on *American Bandstand*. You just have to look groovy. Or I'll be a go-go dancer and dance in a cage.

JANET: In a cage? Like in the zoo?

LILY: Don't be an ignoramus.

JANET: I always thought you would make an excellent teacher.

LILY: 'Cept for the fact that I hate children.

JANET: Don't say *hate*. It doesn't suit you. Take your elbows off the table, sit up straight and eat your dinner. There's children who are starving in Africa who would love that coating.

LILY: Then why don't you mail it to them?

JANET: Jim! We've started!

GRANNY: Is that makeup? You see, Janet?

LILY: No-uh.

GRANNY: There is something shiny and green on your left eyelid.

LILY: We were painting in art class today. Do you have a problem with art, Granny?

GRANNY: And you've got red lipstick on your chin.

LILY: Where?!

GRANNY: There.

LILY: It's a pimple, okay? It's a pimple! It's called acne and teenagers get it and it's really, really awful and you have to point at it and make me feel like a leper! Like it's a blistering boil or something. Were neither of you ever teenagers? You're always picking on me and criticizing me and making me feel like a retard! Everything I do is wrong! My hair is wrong! My skirt is too short! My skirt is not even short – you should see how short Kelly Myers' is. You can't control me forever! If you keep picking on me, maybe I will go wild! Run off with some bikers and do psychedelic drugs and have orgies! How would you like that?

JANET: Lily! No!

GRANNY: If you had been that cheeky when your grandfather was alive he'd have given you a good whack with a leather strap.

LILY: Then it's a good thing he's not around, isn't it?

JANET: Lilibet Wilson. Don't you speak to your grandmother like that. I may not believe in spankings but I will get out the wooden spoon if I need to.

LILY: I hate it here!!

JANET: All right, that's it, young lady – that's going too far!

GRANNY hands JANET the wooden spoon.

LILY: I'm just going to hate it more!

JANET lunges towards LILY. LILY bolts and JANET chases her around the table a couple of times. The phone rings loudly. JANET finally answers it. JIM disappears with a newspaper.

JANET: Wilson residence …. *(Loudly.)* Oh, hi! …We're just having our dinner! But that's fine! Isn't this a surprise! LOVELY to hear from you.

JANET pushes LILY down into her chair where she sits, sulking, picking at her food.

GRANNY: Your mother had a terrible time as a teenager. She was very heavy. Always into the sweets. They used to call her Janet McFatty.

LILY: Figures.

JANET: *(Hand over the phone.)* Would you two be quiet? It's Amy! Long distance!!

GRANNY: Amy?

JANET: *(Into phone.)* Yes, yes!

GRANNY: Tell her I want to talk to her! *(Lower.)* Amy was soo popular. And pretty. Slim hipped. Just like that Twiggy model. And smart as a whip. Head cheerleader *and* valedictorian. Had to fend off the boys with a stick.

JANET: *(Into phone.)* What's that? When did you say?!

LILY: You don't have to shout all the way to San Francisco, Mum.

JANET gives LILY a "kill" look and shushes her with her hand.)

JANET: Pardon, Amy? Lily was distracting me... He is?

GRANNY: *(Low.)* Your mother, on the other hand, didn't have any beaux until she met your father. Not real ones. Sometimes she made boys up and told us she was going out with them but we knew that she was pulling a fast one. Your grandfather used to pretend to be all gruff. "I want to meet that young man before you go out with him," he'd say. But he'd let her go in the end, then we'd have a good laugh.

JANET: *(Into phone)* No, of course we will. We'd be happy to. I am not sure where he's going to sleep; of course, we've got Mum in the guest room now...*(Full of meaning.)* Oh, you know! We have our moments! *(Laughs nervously.)*

GRANNY: It's my turn to speak to Amy.

GRANNY gets up to get the phone.

JANET: Mum wants to speak with you. Do you have a –

GRANNY tries to take the phone away but JANET keeps a firm hand on it.

...All right. Next time....Yes I will....And love to Craig.

GRANNY: I want to speak to her. Amy!!

JANET shakes her head.

Tell her I want to come to San Francisco!

JANET: All right then, Amy.

JANET hangs up.

It was long distance, Mum. You know how expensive that is. If you have something you need to say to Amy you can write her a letter.

GRANNY: I have money and I can pay for the G.D. phone call to my own daughter!

JANET: That money has been put away for a rainy day.

GRANNY: Jim has stolen my money is what he's done.

JANET: *(Low.)* Mother, you know that's not true. He's safely invested it for you. So! Apparently… we are going to get a visit from cousin Robbie!

LILY: Why's he want to come here?

JANET: Amy didn't say. Seems very last minute. He should be here tomorrow night. Maybe he's coming to look at universities.

GRANNY: He's not that old.

JANET: Mum, Robbie's got to be eighteen or nineteen by now.

GRANNY: Is he bringing his stamp collection?

JANET: Oh, the stamp collection! Do you remember, Lily? Stamps from all over the world – Upper Volta and Liechtenstein. If I remember correctly he has a King George stamp, where the head is facing right – only a few were printed. I wonder if he'd bring it in to the IODE? What happened to your stamp collection, Lily?

LILY: I sold it to some drug dealer for a whole bucket of LSD.

JANET: It will be very exciting to see him… Heavens to Gimbels! Jim! Your dinner! Lily, take your father his plate. Of course, silly me, hockey's started.

GRANNY: Well, we won't see him until next May.

LILY: *(As she leaves.)* I'll never get to watch TV now! I hate this house!

JANET: What am I going to make for Robbie? Maybe…ooooh yes….maybe…I should bring out the fondue pot.

GRANNY: Oh goody.

4. What Was That?

Moon Music. The MOONWALKER walks through. JANET looks up for a moment – almost aware of the walker but not. Like a breeze flowing through. GRANNY and LILY are unaware.

5. Am I Sexy?

Music comes out of LILY's portable record player – suggested style: Bobby Sherman's "Little Woman."

LILY stands in front of a mirror. She is examining her body, her hair, and face. She hikes up her skirt very short and tries to look sexy. She slathers some green Pot-o-Shadow on her eyes and Pot-o-Gloss on her lips. She kind of feels herself up as if it were a boy touching her and practises kissing herself in the mirror. Starting to feel something akin to arousal, she takes off her underpants, and sticks a pencil up her skirt, between her legs, masturbating.

JANET: *(Offstage.)* Calling Miss Lily-lumps!

LILY: I'm up!

JANET: *(Offstage.)* Breakfast is almost ready.

LILY: I'm getting dressed! Leave me alone!!

LILY is surprised how good this pencil feels.

JANET: *(Offstage.)* It's Pop Tarts! Just like you asked!

LILY: I'M COMING!!!!

Whoa…this is all too much for LILY. Startled, scared, pleasured…She stops.

JANET: *(Offstage.)* All right! When you deign to give us your presence, your breakfast is in the toaster.

LILY quickly puts her underpants on, lets down her skirt, wipes off the makeup, fixes her hair. She looks at herself in the mirror again. Something has changed.

6. The Wind Changes Direction

JANET, GRANNY, and LILY are playing a game of Mousetrap. Jim is not there.

LILY: Why can't I go?

GRANNY: Whose turn is it?

JANET: I just told you. It's Lily's turn.

GRANNY: She just went.

JANET: No, I just went. I put the bathtub on.

LILY: I still don't get why I can't go. It's just a sock-hop. It's not like anything is going to happen. There'll be teachers there.

JANET: You are too young to be going to boy-girl dances. It's not appropriate. Take your turn.

LILY rolls the die and moves her mouse.

GRANNY: That's my mouse.

LILY: You're blue.

GRANNY: I always take green.

LILY: You always take blue.

JANET: You're blue, Mum.

LILY: Everyone is going.

JANET: If everyone jumped into a pool of sharks, would you?

GRANNY: When are we going to eat dinner?

JANET: You know when. Take your turn.

LILY: I'll ask Daddy, he'll let me go.

JANET: Your father is at poker.

LILY: I'll ask him tomorrow then.

JANET: Is this about the boy who called the other night?

LILY: Maybe.

JANET: The boy helping you with your science project?

GRANNY: I'm hungry. Can I have a Ritz or something?

JANET: No, you can't, it'll ruin your appetite and I've gone to a lot of trouble. Roll, Mother.

GRANNY rolls the die and moves her mouse as:

LILY: I don't want to play this stupid game. When is he going to get here?

GRANNY: You just don't want to play because I'm winning.

JANET: You're not winning, you're losing. Lily is winning.

GRANNY: That's my mouse.

JANET: No it's not, it's Lily's. Yours is blue blue blue blue blue blue!

GRANNY: No need to shout!

Pause.

LILY: Is something burning?

JANET: Oh, for Pete's sake!

JANET runs to the kitchen.

GRANNY: Janet McFatty went to a party and had a farty. That's what the other girls said to your mother.

LILY: That's mean.

GRANNY: Girls *are* mean. Twisting words and telling lies. Boys are so much nicer. They're not as tricky.

As if the wind is gently blowing him in, ROBBIE enters. He is nineteen years old and is a wild, untamed-looking hippie: long hair, bedraggled, psychedelic and absolutely groovy. Perhaps the gentle sound of a sitar.

Lord love a duck. Who's that?

LILY: Oh my gosh, is that Robbie?

GRANNY: That's not Robbie. Robbie has short hair and knobby knees.

ROBBIE: What's happening, Granny-o?

JANET enters.

JANET: Oh, my goodness!! Look who's here!!!

ROBBIE: Aunty J!

JANET: Oh! Oh! Is this what the young people are wearing in San Francisco?

ROBBIE: Only the happening ones, Auntie J.

GRANNY: That's not Robbie.

JANET: It is, Mum, look at his eyes. He's got Amy's eyes.

GRANNY: Amy's eyes aren't red.

JANET: Look at the shape –

GRANNY: Robbie doesn't smell like that.

LILY: Robbie has a scar on his forehead. Remember Uncle Craig clobbered him with a golf club after he poured cereal down the laundry chute? He had all those stitches?

ROBBIE: You're blowing my mind! *(He laughs hysterically.)*

JANET lifts his hair up with the help of the wooden spoon or other implement.

LILY: That's him.

ROBBIE: Who's this little fox?

JANET: That's your cousin, Lilibet.

ROBBIE: Lilibet, far out! Sock it to me, little cuz!

JANET: My goodness. San Francisco must be – !.... You aren't going to love-ins and all that nonsense, are you?

GRANNY: Did you bring your stamp collection, Robbie?

ROBBIE: What? *(He starts laughing hysterically.)* The stamp collection? Granny! That's so far out! This is such a trip!

JANET: And goodness, your parents...what do they think of your hair?

ROBBIE: Mama Bear's cool. The Old Man gets kinda heavy.

JANET: Interesting.

Pause.

And...how long do you plan on staying?

ROBBIE: Just need a pad to crash till I connect with my connectables.

JANET: I was meant to understand it's just for a few days.

ROBBIE: You cool?

JANET: I'd better call your mum and dad, let them know you made it here all right.

ROBBIE: No, Auntie J! No need. Already called the Momster. At the old pay phone.

JANET: Well, I've been holding dinner for you. Are you hungry, Robbie?

ROBBIE: Oh yeaaaaaaaah.

LILY: Mum's made cheese fondue.

JANET: Aaaaand! I've got a tin of Kipper Snacks I am going to open.

ROBBIE: Kipperwhats?

LILY: They're oily little fish that make me gag.

JANET: There's cherry Jell-O for dessert. With fruit slices and marshmallows.

ROBBIE: Jell-O. Right on. Bit of Red Dye Number Two.

GRANNY: What about the roast beef with puddings?

JANET: Lily… *(She gives LILY a meaningful look.)* Can you help me in the kitchen?

JANET and LILY leave. GRANNY stares at ROBBIE with suspicion.

7. Light My Fire

In the basement rec room. LILY is dancing on the couch to The Beach Boys' song: "I Get Around." After a moment, ROBBIE comes in with his beat-up knapsack and guitar case. He flops on the couch. He opens his guitar case, takes out a baggie full of pot from inside the guitar and rolls a joint. LILY turns the music down a bit.

LILY: I met Dennis Wilson once.

ROBBIE: Ya?

LILY: He was here for a concert staying at the Bayshore and I skipped out of school and took the bus downtown and hung out in the lobby all day. He walked through with some girl and they went into a coffee shop and I ordered a glass of apple juice and sat at the table next to them. I had my autograph book with me and I was really wanting to ask him for an autograph but I was so nervous I thought I was going to barf. Then he was finished eating and I knew he was going to leave. He stood up, I stood up, and he looked at me, kinda like he noticed me, and…walked right past. I didn't say anything. I'm such a dunce. But he left crusts of bread from his toast on his plate and I brought them home. They're kind of fossilized now.

ROBBIE: Huh.

ROBBIE lights the joint and takes a deep toke.

LILY: Is that marijuana?

ROBBIE: Maui Wowie. Wanna toke? It'll blow your mind.

LILY: I don't think so. My mum would have a bird if she knew. She gets hysterical if I say the word *cigarette*. But she hardly ever comes down here since we put the laundry off the kitchen... The couch is super soft, you're going to sleep really well down here...

The record is over now and LILY is looking for another one.

Do you like Anne Murray? Have you heard "Snowbird"?

ROBBIE: Canadians are all square. Except for the Trudeau man. He's where it's at. "The state has no place in the bedrooms of the nation." Right on, brother! That is so outta sight! Hangin' loose with John and the Yoko-Lady – I am sure those three smoked some wild weed.

LILY: I wish I could vote so I could vote for Mr. Trudeau because he's a swinger. He went out with Barbra Streisand. My mum always says she's too busy to vote but if she did vote, even though she liked Mr. Trudeau when everyone was throwing flowers at him, she would vote the way my dad votes and my dad says Mr. Trudeau wants to shove French down our throats and is a Nancy-boy and a communist to boot. My mum and dad are really, really square.

ROBBIE picks up his guitar and strums a few chords, plays a few riffs. Still smoking the joint.

Wow, you play guitar.

ROBBIE starts to play a song he has written, sounding very much like Bob Dylan. LILY sits at his feet.

Robbie (Tony Adams) opens the mind of his cousin Lily (Katie Ryerson) to the possibilities of a new and complicated world.

Photo by Andrew Alexander.

ROBBIE: *(Singing)* There's a new wind a-blowin'
Blowin' with change
It starts with you, oh baby
And it starts with me too.
It's time to make a difference, people
We need to be standin' tall
Not acting so small
The pigs will win if we let 'em in,
And the world will lose in the end.
There's a new wind a-blowin'
Blowin' with change
It starts with you, oh baby,
And it starts with me too.
Freedom won't come easy,
Doesn't come with guns and war
And it doesn't...
Freedom don't come easy...and it doesn't...

ROBBIE can't remember the next words. He stops playing, then gets lost in his mind for a moment. He's stoned for sure.

LILY: So...are you an actual hippie?

ROBBIE: Definition request.

LILY: A hippie. You know.

ROBBIE: I have a spirit that's free, a mind that is tangled with thought and ideas. I lost my virginity in an alley around the corner from Haight and Ashbury during the Summer of Love. I crossed the land in a VW van that was painted with turquoise flowers of power and psychedelic swirls. Danced naked to the waist in the mud at Woodstock. Tie-dyed shirts that are purple and orange and burnt my hands while batiking with wax. I have carried placards that read "Fuck the Pigs" and "Make Love Not War" and "Black is Beautiful." I've seen the great Janis Joplin shoot three bags of heroin directly into her veins and have passed the Acid Test thirty-two times. I have joined be-ins, love-ins, sit-ins, peace-ins. Made crowns of daisies and beads of love. I believe in the words of Ginsberg and Kerouac. I have experienced Hinduism and Buddhism, chanted with Hare Krishnas and popped peyote buttons with a Navajo tribe. I denounce materialism, authority, institutions, conventions and constrictions. I defy simple labels. Can ya dig it?

Short pause.

LILY: Wowa.

Pause.

So why... Why'd you come here? To Vancouver?

ROBBIE: Going to find my way to a commune. Back to the land. Back to stardust. Grow my own food. My own grass. Live with the people. Do my own thing. Make lots and lots of love, not war...

LILY: That's sooo cool. Maybe I can visit you there.

Pause.

ROBBIE takes an album out of his knapsack and puts it on. It's psychedelic and groovy. He starts grooving to the music.

You're a really good dancer. I'm going to be a go-go dancer one day... Maybe.

ROBBIE keeps dancing in his own world. LILY climbs onto the couch and starts dancing like a go-go girl. After a bit she hops off the couch and begins to imitate his cool dancing. He starts to dance with her, slightly suggestively. He kisses her sweetly on the lips. She moves away, a little bit shocked but kind of liking it. He looks at her and starts to kiss her again; she doesn't stop him at first and then does.

ROBBIE: Hey Lilikins. You a virgin, girl?

LILY: I am not a virgin.

ROBBIE: Oh yes, you are….how old are you?

LILY: Old enough. I went to third base with a boy at school.

ROBBIE: Oh, Baby. Third base is not the sweet deal. Not the sweet deal at all.

ROBBIE starts to move in on LILY again.

And….. you…Miss Lilikins…. are going to like it soooo much.

ROBBIE kisses LILY, harder this time, tongues might be involved. LILY pulls away.

LILY: Oh my gosh! I just remembered, I have all this homework to do.

LILY scoots out of the rec room. ROBBIE grooves to the music.

8. The Earth Quakes

Breakfast. JIM is not in his usual spot. GRANNY sits at the table. JANET serves her some porridge. GRANNY stares at it for a moment, pokes it.

JANET: Lily, breakfast!

JANET mixes up some Tang as:

GRANNY: What's this?

JANET: It's your porridge, Mum.

GRANNY: *(Suspicious.)* Hmmmmm.

JANET: What's wrong with it?

Pause.

Mum?

GRANNY: Can't I have my usual breakfast?

JANET: This *is* your usual breakfast. You've had porridge every morning since you got here.

GRANNY: That's an exaggeration.

JANET: Every *single* morning. I've offered you Shredded Wheat, puffed rice, Bran Buds and you always want porridge.

GRANNY: I don't like porridge. I like toad-in-a-hole.

JANET: If you don't like porridge, then you should have told me. I am not a mind reader, you know. If you had told me, then I wouldn't have gone to the trouble of making the dashed stuff.

GRANNY: All right, don't get all worked up.

JANET: Well!

JANET takes the porridge away. LILY enters. She's looking a little bit groovy. Her hair has been straightened, she is wearing makeup and her skirt is short. GRANNY immediately notices the makeup and is about to squeal when:

LILY: *(Low to GRANNY.)* Don't you dare make a fuss or I'll tell Mum about your "little accident" in the bathroom.

JANET gives LILY a bowl and the box of Lucky Charms.

JANET: My goodness. Lily! All dressed up on a Saturday morning? *(Teasing.)* Seeing a special someone from your science class?

LILY: Mum!

GRANNY: I know who she's dressed up for! It's unnatural!

LILY elbows GRANNY in the ribs.

Ow!

ROBBIE enters.

ROBBIE: Hey, Auntie J, do I detect some groovy breakfast smells?

JANET: Here's the man of the hour. How'd you sleep, Mr. San Francisco?

ROBBIE: Like a babe in a basket of weeds.

LILY: Hi, Robbie.

ROBBIE: Hey…foxy lady.

JANET: How does porridge sound?

ROBBIE: Right on! I haven't had porridge since the Stone Ages.

JANET: Well, that's good, because Granny McPicky doesn't want her perfectly good porridge.

JANET gives ROBBIE GRANNY's porridge. He stares at the bowl.

ROBBIE: That is blowing my mind.

JANET: What?

ROBBIE: The lady with the crown looking at me.

JANET: Queen Elizabeth at age thirty-two. Our very own Queen of Canada, who, as it happens –

The phone rings loudly and JANET answers it.

Wilson residence… Oh hi, Craig –

ROBBIE looks up.

– yes, he's arrived safe and sound. I'm planning to fatten him up with a nice roast of beef tonight –

Pause.

Pardon me?

Pause.

I don't like your tone here, Craig. Not one bit.

Pause.

Robbie?

Pause.

No, I most certainly did not know that. I had no idea…

LILY looks up with interest. Long pause, dotted with:

I see… I see…

Well, I am sure Amy meant well…

GRANNY: Amy?

Pause.

JANET: No, of course he should. I would agree.

Pause.

Yes, I'll get him. Just a minute…Robbie, it's your father on the phone…

ROBBIE is paralyzed, everyone looks at him.

ROBBIE: *(Low.)* I can't…tell him I'm out… Gone to see the fish.

JANET puts her hand over the receiver.

JANET: Come over here and speak to your father. He's waiting.

ROBBIE: I'll call him back, I've gotta –

ROBBIE moves like he might leave the room.

JANET: Robert!

(Into phone.) He's right here, Craig.

JANET holds out the receiver. ROBBIE takes the phone.

ROBBIE: Yes, sir?

JANET quietly busies herself with breakfast cleanup.

Yes, sir. I understand, sir, but –

LILY: Why does he call his father "sir"? That's so weird.

JANET: Lily, why don't you go watch TV?

Robbie (Tony Adams) speaks to his oppressive father on the phone as his aunt Janet (Marion Day), Granny (Beverley Wolfe) and cousin Lily (Katie Ryerson) look on.

Photo by Andrew Alexander.

LILY: What's going on, Mum? What's Uncle Craig want?

JANET: Just do as I say for once!

LILY: All right!! Don't go all mental!

LILY goes. She watches TV as:

ROBBIE: Yes, sir.

ROBBIE's stance changes as his mother comes on the line.

Mom?... Why did you tell him...?

GRANNY: Is that Amy on the phone? Tell her I want to come to San Francisco.

JANET: Not now, Mum.

GRANNY: It's like a prison here!

JANET: Listen, I am going to make an appointment with Dr. Honeywell, maybe he can help.

GRANNY: Help what?

JANET: Calm you down a bit.

GRANNY: I don't need calming down. I am so calmed down in this house I am practically dead already!!

JANET: Shush!

They are all quiet, watching ROBBIE. After a moment, ROBBIE lowers the phone, holding it to his chest, as he considers what he has just heard. JANET takes the phone.

JANET: Amy? Are you still there?... Now, stop crying…it'll all work out for the best… Amy?… Craig, I have a right to talk to my sister!

The phone has gone dead at the other end. JANET pauses before she hangs up. She looks at ROBBIE.

Well, now.

Pause.

I guess I have a draft dodger for a nephew.

ROBBIE: It's going to be all groovy, Aunty J.

JANET: It is certainly not groovy. You are breaking the law.

ROBBIE: I'll land as an immigrant here. They said at the border. Lester B and the Trudeau man are lookin' out for me. You Canadians are cool.

JANET: You could never go back. They'd put you in jail.

ROBBIE: I'd rather be alive than at the end of stick roasted by the fucking Viet Cong.

JANET: No need for language.

ROBBIE: There is need for language, Auntie Janet. Big bad language! Because this is my fucking life we are talking about! You know what happed to the poor shit Louie Piper that lives down the street from us? First day in Nam, the Cong blows both his legs off. First day! He used to play football and had cheerleaders sitting in his lap. Now he has no lap. He just has two stumps, drinks until he pukes. Only twenty years old and his life's fucking over. That's not my scene!

JANET: Lower your voice, we don't need the whole neighbourhood hearing your foulness.

ROBBIE: You gotta know it's crazy over there.

JANET: During the Second World War – what would have happened if we hadn't stopped the Germans? Hmmm? What would have happened if all the young men turned and ran? Hitler'd be running the show.

ROBBIE: Vietnam is not the Third Reich. Nobody has any idea why we're there.

JANET: All those communists! The Russians and the Chinese – they've got to be stopped!

LILY turns the TV down so she can listen. GRANNY notices ROBBIE's bowl of uneaten porridge and begins to eat it.

ROBBIE: Auntie Janet – please don't get uptight about this. Mom is cool. She gave me the bread to come. She said "Go to Auntie J's, crash with her, she'll take care of you."

JANET: Oh she did, did she?

ROBBIE: And here you are taking care of me. Cooking all these sweet meals. I'm sure the Momster will come for a visit or two. Nice to have some sister time? And I'll help out, mow the lawn, that type of thing.

GRANNY: What's that? Robbie's staying? Is he taking the guest room? Where am I going to go? I am not going with the droolers! You won't have my money if you send me to those droolers!

ROBBIE: Hang loose, Granny! You don't need to bother with me. I'll lay low in the basement.

JANET: You will not be staying in my house. I will not harbour a criminal.

ROBBIE: I'm hip, I'll hang with the beach crowd. Tent up. Or head inland. Do my own thing.

JANET: Do your own thing? Wouldn't we all like to do our own thing. And what would happen to the world if all of us did our own things? Laundry would never get done. People would never eat. We all need to do our duty, Robert. Even you. You must stand by the other young men who are serving their country instead of running away like a coward.

ROBBIE: No, no, Auntie J –

JANET: Your father wants you to come home to face your responsibilities. He was furious when he heard that you'd left and that…Amy had given you money to go! *(Low.)* And where does this leave your mother? She can't cross her husband like that without…serious consequences. You know that better than I do.

ROBBIE collapses.

ROBBIE: *(To himself.)* No no no no no no no….

JANET: Your mum and dad'll be leaving shortly. They will be here late tomorrow. That's good. Better to get it over with.

GRANNY: They have lemon trees in San Francisco.

Pause.

ROBBIE: And gentle people weeping…

JANET: *(Low.)* Now don't you think about leaving this house. You know what he'll do to your mother if you're not here when they arrive.

JANET takes ROBBIE's hand and pats it.

It's going to be fine, Robbie, you'll see. Everything will be fine.

9. There's Something Out There

Moon Music. The MOONWALKER (played by the actor who plays LILY this time) moves through the space. ROBBIE, GRANNY, and LILY don't notice it but JANET does; she raises her head, not seeing but feeling the MOONWALKER's presence.

10. Things Are Out of Control

LILY enters the rec room where ROBBIE is sitting cross-legged on the couch. He's meditating.)

LILY: Robbie….?

ROBBIE opens his eyes but stares straight ahead.

What's going on? Are you going to Vietnam?... How do you get drafted?

Pause.

ROBBIE: They do it by birthdays. Trying to make it all fair. Tricky Dick Nixon had this bright idea to have it on TV. So instead of watching *Andy of Mayberry*, the whole country watched the Draft Lottery: buncha old Republicans in suits and glasses pulling numbers out of a big glass jar, deciding who is going to be drafted first.

Some of my buddies got together that night and dropped acid to watch. I planned to hang loose with them but my father, who is one serious dude, ordered me to sit and watch that lottery "like a man for once in my shit-filled life or he'd pin me down and hack off my girlie hair with his bowie knife." So the three of us, Mom, Big Man Daddy-o, and me, sat in front of the television set; nice little family party. I was freaking out on the inside but sitting up "like a man" on the outside.

They had this bright idea to invite the youth of the country to pick out capsules. So this absolutely square dude, Paul Murray, whose a member of The – get this – Selective Service Youth Advisory Council – steps up to the jar to draw out a buncha capsules. Puts his hand in, picks the first one he touches, hands it to Suit-man. Suit-man opens it, tugs out the paper, unrolls it, reads it out loud. The first birth date they picked was September 14th. So all the poor losers born on September 14 were the first to be called up. Suit-man pinned that date up by the number 001. Paul Murray dips his hand back in the cookie jar, comes up with a second date. April, 24th. My birthday. I am draft number 002.

My old man leans over, puts his hand on my shoulder with that firm grip he has and says, "Congratulations, son, you are going to make your country proud." Mom goes all pale like mashed potatoes. Tears splurting out, mouth all crumpled…I stand, start walking, out the door, barefoot, into the California breeze. I let that breeze take me right down to Haight Ashbury and the world of psychedelic bliss. Was trippin' for a week.

LILY: Wow. What a bummer.

ROBBIE: Mom seeks me out, says, "Go to Canada." Land of her youth. Home of the wild and the free. And family. Supposed to keep me safe.

LILY: Don't listen to my mother. You can't go back. You've got to go somewhere and hide. Maybe at that commune you were talking about... I've got some babysitting money you can have.

ROBBIE: My father promised to smash each of my mom's toes with a claw hammer, one for every day I am AWOL. And that fucker is a man of his word. My goose is officially cooked.

LILY is teary. She sits down close to ROBBIE. She puts her head on his shoulder. ROBBIE smells her hair. He leans in and kisses LILY, gently at first and then more eagerly. After a moment LILY pulls away.

LILY: Isn't it weird that we're cousins?

ROBBIE: That's just what the shitheads *want* you to believe. They want to make it dirty but it's all so beautiful.

ROBBIE kisses LILY again, pushing her back onto the couch. His hand moves under her top.

LILY: *(Pulling away and sitting up.)* I don't know if I am ready for this experience yet.

ROBBIE: Ohhh...you are so ready, baby. Sex is going to blow your mind.

(Moving in.) And you don't know how bad I need this right now.

LILY: I don't think so, Robbie. I'm only fifteen.

ROBBIE: I'll take good care of you, little cuz. You don't need to do a thing... Let me do it all. I will liberate you.

He moves very slowly and gently at first, his hands moving on her. Kissing her gently. LILY starts to pull away as he presses in on her, pushing her down on the couch, getting on top of her. He starts to undo his pants. LILY is squirming, trying to get away.

LILY: No! No! I don't want to.

ROBBIE: I need this so bad. Don't stop me now. We are going to go straight to the moon.

LILY pushes him off!

LILY: Robbie, stop!!

ROBBIE: Jeeesus!

He pulls back.

We've gone too far. You've got to finish me off.

LILY: What?

ROBBIE: I'll teach you. Your boyfriends will thank me for it.

ROBBIE undoes his belt and pulls LILY's hand towards his crotch. Blackout. Transitional Music up: Suggested style: "For What it's Worth" by Buffalo Springfield, bleeding into:

11. All Good Things Must Come to an End

Front porch of the Wilson home: JANET, LILY, and GRANNY stand looking out. GRANNY has her coat on and holds a small travelling suitcase. LILY is sulking, not making eye contact. JANET has a fixed smile. We hear the sounds of a car trunk opening and closing under:

GRANNY: Where's Amy?

JANET: She didn't come, Mother. She's not feeling well.

GRANNY: Just Craig?

JANET: He's come to take Robbie home to San Francisco.

GRANNY: But not me?

JANET: No.

Sound of car doors opening and closing.

Robbie is going to Vietnam.

GRANNY: What for?

JANET: You know very well why he's going…He's going to become a man. Serve his country. Make us proud.

Car starts up. JANET waves good-bye. As the car pulls away, LILY suddenly explodes.

LILY: Robbieeeeeeee!!!!!!

JANET: Lily! What on earth…?

LILY goes back into the house.

GRANNY: There was a wild animal in the house last night. Groaning and moaning. Did you hear it?

Transitional music. Suggested style: "Lay Lady Lay" by Bob Dylan.

12. Let's Have a Heart to Heart

LILY is curled in a ball on the couch in the basement, makeup smudged from crying. JANET comes and sits by her. She holds a book.

JANET: Sweetheart. We need to have a little chat.

No response.

I know things are a little confusing at the moment. Your father so busy with work. Granny coming to live with us. Robbie coming and going. Uncle Craig… But I wanted to let you know that everything is going work out for the best. And in the meantime, you are turning into a young lady right before my very eyes. You're fifteen now, next year you'll be sixteen… After that you'll be seventeen… Things are changing very quickly. You want to go to sock hops and mixers with boys. You want to wear makeup and short skirts. Boys are calling you on the telephone… Lily, I've got something for you to read. Dr. Honeywell gave it to me. It's a lovely little booklet that explains everything you need to know about being a woman.

LILY looks at her mother. JANET hands LILY a small book.

It's called *Growing up and Liking It*.

LILY takes the book, looks at it, then opens it to the first page.

JANET: *(Reading.)* "The fun is just beginning."

Her duty done, JANET stands to leave.

LILY: Mum?

JANET: Yes?

Pause.

What is it, sweetheart?

Pause.

LILY: Nothing.

JANET: Well, you read that and after, if you have any questions, I'll make an appointment for you to speak with Dr. Honeywell. All right?

JANET moves to go.

Oh, by the way. I bought you a new box of Kotex pads. They're in the bathroom closet, tucked behind the towels. Bigger ones. Supers.

JANET leaves. LILY drops the book and curls up again.

13. Things Are Getting Out of Control

Moon Music: the man in the space suit is back. Only this time the MOONWALKER walks a bit on the moon and then seems to lose control, flying off into the galaxy, into nothingness. JANET watches this happen. LILY raises her head, not seeing him but feeling something.

Music transition takes us out. Suggested style: "War" by Edwin Starr.

End of Act One.

Act Two

Spring, Vancouver – 1971.

14. Nuts to That

We see the MOONWALKER move in space as: we hear a riotous sound montage of news reporting: newscasters touching briefly on some of events of early 1971 such as: Canada adopting multiculturalism, tobacco companies announcing they will place health warnings on cigarette packages, oil tankers colliding, Charles Manson convicted, busing/racial issues in the States, fallout from Trudeau implementing the October Crisis, Trudeau's recent marriage to Margaret Sinclair, the latest casualty numbers from the war in Vietnam, one-year anniversary of Kent State, fallout from the disastrous Apollo 13. The sounds fade as:

Lights come up on JANET in full craft-making mode: there is a basket of red and white flowers. She is making them out of tissue paper, green pipe cleaners, and sticky green tape.

JANET: *(Under her breath, by rote.)* Divorced, beheaded, died; divorced, beheaded, survived. Catherine of Aragon, Anne Boleyn, Jane Seymour, Anne of Cleeves, Catherine Howard, Catherine Parr. All. Boys. Should. Come. Home. Please.

(To "her audience.") I've always been very proud that Dad's father's father was in Royal Service. Starting out at Marlborough House as Nursery Footman, then Cellarman, Messenger under the watch of the Lord Chamberlain, all the way up to Postmaster to Queen Victoria. Great-grandfather met his second wife when she was a maid to Princess Mary. Mary was the sister of Edward, George, and the prince who was a bit odd and got sent up to Sandringham for safekeeping.

As a young Janet Underwood, I used to wish I could parlay my family connections to get my own position at Buckingham Palace...then of course I met Jim and became Mrs. James Wilson.

She finishes a flower.

But now *(Secretive smile.)*...it looks like Buckingham Palace is coming to me.

She starts making another flower.

I won't even listen to those naysayers who put down the monarchy; "Charles hasn't done well at his O levels"; "there's Margaret in a restaurant with a divorced man." Nuts to that. Look at Elizabeth and Philip. Supporting each other. Encouraging each other. Loving each other.

It's the same naysayers who pooh-pooh the space missions. But I say it's worth it, just for the excitement. The dreams. Man has actually walked on the moon three times! Apollo 13 didn't go so well, but they made it back to Earth, safe and sound, so in the end it all worked out just fine. And then Apollo 14 went so smoothly; dashingly handsome Alan Shepard making that impeccable landing of the Module Antares. And! The clever man had the brilliant idea to bring a Wilson six-iron attached to a lunar-sample-scoop-handle, which made a perfectly perfect golf club. Even in that great white space suit, he managed to hit a ball that went for miles and miles and miles. Across the soft, dusty terrain of the moon. Bouncing over craters, into the dark shadows of mystery.

We may all be going to the moon ourselves one day… Wouldn't be surprised if Queen Elizabeth herself decided to make the journey. Conquering new realms. Waving at her moon people. I might be there too…walking on the moon, completely weightless… Lovely idea, really… Lovely…

Moon Music. We see the MOONWALKER in the shadows. JANET is distracted by his presence, and pricks her finger with a pipe cleaner, drawing a spot of blood.

Ouch! Dash it.

The MOONWALKER is gone. GRANNY sits in a chair, a cane by her side, frailer than before. She's fallen asleep with a half-made flower on her lap. JANET wipes the blood off her finger with a tissue.

JANET: Mother. Wake up. Festive flowers don't make themselves.

GRANNY: Hmmmm?

JANET: Your petals are too big. You need to look at the prototype. You see?

Janet (Marion Day) makes red and paper flowers to line the handrails in preparation for the Queen's royal visit. Granny (Beverley Wolfe) tries to help.

Photo by Martin Conboy.

GRANNY: I had such a garden. With real flowers that I cut and put in Mason jars so they filled the house with their honeyed smells. Not these fakers. What good are phony flowers?

JANET: We're going to decorate the handrails all the way into the airport. A sea of red and white.

GRANNY: Hmm?

JANET: For the Royal Visit.

GRANNY: The what?

JANET: Heavens to Gimbels, what have I been talking about for the past six months? Queen Elizabeth is coming with Philip and Anne. For BC's centenary. The Dunbar Chapter of the Imperial Order Daughters of the Empire has been asked to help with the celebrations and of course, you know *very* well, that I, as newly anointed head of the chapter, have been asked to present a bouquet of flowers to Her Majesty the Queen herself.

GRANNY: So we're making bogus blooms for those horse-traders ?

JANET: Yes and we've got several hundred more to go, so get cracking.

JANET starts flower making again.

I've asked each member of the IODE to fill a quota, so we have to keep up our end. I mean the Royal Party is arriving this weekend! Sheila Witherspoon has absolutely refused to be helpful. She's as cold as an Eskimo in a North Pole igloo. Practically delirious with jealousy.

GRANNY: I once was in an igloo. It was warm and cozy.

JANET: It's not my fault that I happen to become president of the IODE the very year of the Royal Visit.

GRANNY halfheartedly starts working on her flower.

GRANNY: Amy's wedding had the most beautiful flowers. Her bouquet fresh…yellow roses… white daisies. Gentlemen with perfect buds in the lapels of their tuxedos. The girls, bunches of pink and yellow daisies. An archway of cedar boughs. Cost us a bundle. The wedding had all those frat boys at it, doing their frat boy chants during the toasts. They were a laugh riot. I thought I was going to piddle my undies. Craig was Sigma Chi. Now THAT was something to remember. Yours and Jim's wasn't nearly so big. You got married so suddenly. City Hall! And slam, bam, before you know it, Lily arrived.

JANET: I got pregnant on my wedding night and she was several weeks early, so it was quite the whirlwind.

GRANNY: Didn't look early at all. Big healthy baby. You were never good at math.

JANET: Jim and I met at –

GRANNY: Craig and Amy's house is surrounded by bushes of pink bougainvillea. They grow avocados. Pluck lemons and oranges right out of trees in their own back yard. That's San Francisco. Happy as two peas in a sweet pea pod.

JANET: *(To herself.)* I wouldn't be too sure about that.

GRANNY: Jim home tonight?

JANET: I believe it's a Shriner's bowling night.

GRANNY: He's been promising to change that light bulb in my room for three weeks.

JANET: You know I just read a very good article in a magazine. "Ten Tips for a Perfect Marriage." One of their very good suggestions is finding things you and your hubby can do together. So I'm going to propose we both take up golf! I called up Point Grey Golf Club to see what lessons cost and –

GRANNY: Golf? With Jim? And you? Wake me up when you stop dreaming.

JANET: Mother! Do you need one of your pills?

GRANNY: He clearly can't stand being around you. He's never home. Neither is whatshername.

JANET: *Lily* has a meeting. Mrs. MacPherson – the Home Economics teacher – has started a new club, just for the girls. It will be good for her to learn some practical skills.

GRANNY: I wish she'd go back to wearing makeup. She looks like one of those old rubbies down on Hastings.

JANET: I'm going to make a pot of tea.

GRANNY: Orange pekoe?

JANET: I think I'll make Earl Grey today.

GRANNY: Tastes like soap.

JANET: Earl Grey it is.

JANET opens a cupboard. The MOONWALKER's head can be seen through the back of the cupboard. There's a box of chocolates. She opens it up and tries to eat one without her mother seeing.

GRANNY: That chocolate will go right to your hips.

JANET hides her chocolate.

JANET: What are you talking about, Mum? Are you having one of your spells?

GRANNY: You'll never attract a nice young man with those massive hips of yours. Boys like slim-hipped girls.

JANET: Mum! I am not a young girl any more, I am a woman. You're muddled again.

GRANNY: It's always the dirty ones lurking about you.

JANET: I'm going to get your pills.

GRANNY: I'm not taking those pills. They bung me up.

JANET: Then I'll buy you some prunes. C'mon, Mum, I'm going to pop it right into your mouth. Here we go. Now open up the garage door, open up. Say a big "ahhhhh."

GRANNY: Ahhhhhh.

JANET pops the pill in and gives GRANNY a glug of water. GRANNY swallows. JANET wipes the dribbling water from her mother's chin.

JANET: There you go. That's better.

JANET goes about making the tea, as LILY, now seventeen, comes into the kitchen and gets herself a snack. She wears scruffy, patched jeans, and a shirt with a vest; her hair is long and straight. She's holding a bunch of books, including Love Story.

How was school?

LILY: I have to write a stupid book report. I tried to say that I don't have to write a report to prove I know the story. I've seen the movie about ten times. I can quote half of it by heart. "What can you say about a twenty-five-year-old girl who died?"

JANET: Okay, okay.

LILY: "Love means never having to say you're sorry. Right, preppie?"

JANET: Well, when you are finished your report, I'd like some help with these flowers.

LILY: Why do I have to help? I don't even like all this royal family B.S. We're all supposed to make a fuss about them because they happened to be born into the "right" family and they have a lot of money and wear fancy tiaras? That's really bourgeois.

JANET: Listen to me, young lady, I wouldn't be getting so cheeky when you've got a birthday right around the corner, gifts can be returned.

LILY: The Queen wouldn't even be that important if she had an older brother. Talk about a patriarchy.

JANET: A what?

LILY: It's high time we stopped giving all the power to men. We're 50% of the population with zero percentage of the power. Men hate women: they don't know they hate them, but they do. But they hate themselves even more. That's why they want to keep us barefoot in the kitchen. Turn us into their cooking, cleaning sex slaves.

JANET: Sex slaves!! What is going on here? Lily!

LILY: Ms. Cluninger says that it's up to my generation to change things.

JANET: For heaven's sake, who is Miss Cluninger?

LILY: *Mssssss* Cluninger. It used to be Mrs. MacPherson but she doesn't want to be labelled as some man's wife anymore. So she's taken back the name she was born with, and she says Mizz instead of Missus. Because she doesn't want to be any man's property, she's rejecting the roles that everyone wants to box her into. She told her whole family to make their own meals and clean their own toilets. And that she was going to be wearing pants from now on because she was sick and tired of enduring the chains of garters and girdles. Women have to take control of their own bodies and have abortions whenever they want to. They have to reject the traditional roles of the suburban housewife with its consumerist repression that forces women to be sexual eunuchs. I am never getting married. Ever. Ms. Cluninger's a big women's libber and I think she is so right on.

JANET: Is this… what the new after-school club is all about?

LILY: It's a consciousness-raising group. We're going to start a revolution. She's challenged us to join her and burn our bras of repression and celebrate our bodies by drinking our menstrual blood.

JANET pales and has to sit down. She tries to speak but can't.

All men are male chauvinist pigs. Even Dad.

JANET: Lilibet!

LILY: And Uncle Craig – he's a monster. I don't know why Aunt Amy doesn't leave him.

JANET: Leave him? Where would she go?

LILY: I don't know. Robbie told me he hits her, all the time. Uncle Craig was going to break all her bones if Robbie didn't go back. That's the only reason he's in stupid Vietnam now.

JANET: These are not things…to be discussed…like this.

JANET gets up and starts looking for something in the kitchen cupboards. Moon Music sneaks in under:

And certainly not something to be talked about outside this house. You hear me?

LILY: If women were running the world, there wouldn't even be wars and Robbie wouldn't be over in Vietnam. You should never have made him go.

JANET: Stop this!! Stop it right now!! I will not discuss any of this any further. And when your father gets home –

LILY: When Dad gets home? When is Dad ever home? Don't be such a spaz! His life doesn't include us. I don't think he even knows what I look like. The last time I actually heard him speak to me was two years ago when he told me to get my hair out of my eyes.

JANET: What has got into you?

LILY: Sense. That is what has got into me. Sense. And if you don't want to talk to me about things that are important, if you don't want to hear what I have to say, then I won't even bother trying.

LILY sits in front of the TV and turns on All in the Family. *The MOONWALKER's arm comes out of a cupboard, handing JANET a bottle of sherry, which she secretly adds to her tea and takes a sip. Moon Music fades away.*

JANET: I just don't understand that girl! She's so emotional these days. I've heard about teenagers, but this is the limit!

JANET looks at her mother. GRANNY is asleep again.

Perhaps it's just a phase.

Heavens to Gimbels, look at the time. I've got to get the sheets ironed and the bed made before dinner.

She puts her flower-making away.

Goodness…

JANET notices her hands, the palms are covered in red dye, from the tissue paper.

15. The World Is Encroaching on My Kitchen

Moon Music. The MOONWALKER is seen again, holding the American Flag, only this time the flag is burnt and tattered. Instead of his helmet he wears an M17 gas mask, like the ones issued to soldiers during the Vietnam War.

16. I Don't Know Who My Daughter Is

JANET and LILY sit at the kitchen table, which is set for four. GRANNY is asleep in a chair, with a paper napkin tucked into her collar. LILY has a large peace symbol on a chain around her neck and wears a bandana around her head. There is a balloon attached to the back of LILY's chair. On it, in marker, is printed "Happy Birthday Lily!" A cake with candles sits on the counter, but the candles have not been lit. There are baskets of red and white flowers. JANET's hands now are completely red, she has a cloth and is trying to wipe off the dye.

JANET: Three days until… What will Her Majesty think if she sees…?

Perhaps if I soak them in bleach.

LILY: How long are we going to have to wait for him?

JANET: We could play a game of spoons.

LILY rolls her eyes.

I know, let's get the old Twister game out.

LILY: Are you mental?

He doesn't even care that it's my birthday. He doesn't care about anybody but his poker buddies, his idiotic Shriner friends and his new –

Short pause.

JANET: His new what?

LILY: Nothing.

Can't I at least open a present? I'm not sitting *here* all night. I've got things to do.

JANET: He promised he'd be home in time for cake.

LILY: He promised? Dream on.

Phone rings.

JANET: That's probably him now.

JANET turns off the music and answers it.

Wilson residence... Hi, dear, you on your way? We've finished dinner and are holding the cake... Oh no!... Well...how long will you be?... Jim!... Do you want to speak to the birthday girl?... All right. I understand. We'll see you when we see you. *(Remembering.)* Oh, Jim, don't forget that Saturday is the big day, so you'll need to –

But JIM is gone. JANET hangs up the phone, gets the matches and starts lighting the candles on the cake.

LILY: What's his excuse this time?

JANET: Your father has to go over a few things with the new secretary. Apparently there's a big logjam at work that has to be dealt with tonight and he's not sure what time he's going to be home.

LILY: And you believe him?

JANET: Of course I believe him, why shouldn't I believe him? Don't be cheeky.

LILY: What did I say?

JANET: You had that look.

LILY: I'm getting in trouble for my *looks* now? I don't believe it. You're the one who's always giving me the hairy eyeball.

JANET: All right, all right. Well, he sends you a hundred birthday kisses. Make a wish and blow out the candles… Seventeen, how time flies.

LILY thinks for a moment then blows them out.

Ohhhh…I'd give my eyetooth to know what you wished for… Something nice, I hope.

LILY: If you really want to know what I wished for, I'll tell you. I wished that your generation would stop wrecking the world so we could have world peace and harmony.

Beat.

JANET: Now! There's a few presents here for a certain birthday girl. One from me and your dad. *(Looks for a gift.)*

LILY: Yeah, right.

JANET hands LILY a wrapped record. LILY shakes it.

(Teasing.) Hmmm. I wonder what this is.

JANET: No guessing, now.

LILY: I'm sure it's a book.

JANET: Careful, I can reuse that paper.

LILY opens the present. It's a Beach Boys album. A disappointed silence.

LILY: Thanks, Mum.

JANET: Do you want to play it?

LILY: That's okay.

JANET: Let me put it on for you. I know you love your Beach Boys.

LILY: *Did*...love the Beach Boys. Their music is kind of for babies. It's not about anything. Everyone is having fun driving around in cars and kissing on the beach?? Duh.

JANET: Music doesn't have to be about anything, it's music.

JANET looks for another present as:

LILY: Music to my generation is like what the Bible is to yours.

(Singing with mucho emotion.)
"I am woman, hear me roar,
In numbers too big to ignore,
And I know too much to go back an' pretend"

JANET: Mum, wake up. Lily's going to open your present.

JANET pokes GRANNY, who wakes with a start.

LILY: *(Singing.)* "'Cause I've heard it all before
And I've been down there on the floor
No one's ever gonna keep me down again"

JANET: Mother. It's Lily's birthday. She's opening that present you wanted to give her. Perk up.

LILY: *(Singing.)* "I am strong, I am invincible, I am woooooman"...

JANET pushes a large box towards LILY. LILY slowly opens it as she speaks.

Ms. Cluninger's organized us to go to a protest. Did you know that the United States has been testing nuclear bombs off the coast of BC?

JANET: I suppose they have to test bombs somewhere.

LILY: Are you joking?

JANET: Okay…look at what your granny is giving you.

GRANNY: What am I giving her?

LILY: What if they start an earthquake? What if radiation leaks out? Who's going to be affected? Us! We'll get radiation sickness, the plants will all die. Or worse, we'll all be melting like wax.

JANET: Open the box, Lily.

LILY fiddles with tape on the box.

LILY: Stupid Richard Nixon doesn't give a crap about Canadians. And then that jerk John Wayne pulls into the harbour in his luxury yacht, and you know what he says?

JANET: *(Warning.)* I happen to like John Wayne. He was very good in *True Grit.*

GRANNY: He's no Clark Gable.

LILY: He says that anyone who disagrees with the testing is a bunch of commies who should mind their own business.

GRANNY: I once went to a meeting of communists.

LILY: You did?

GRANNY: I thought they had some very interesting ideas; everyone having enough to eat, for example.

JANET: Isn't that the limit.

LILY: I'd rather be a communist than a soul-sucking capitalist.

JANET: Open the bloody gift!

LILY: The protest is tonight. We're going to stop them if we have to rent a boat and go out on the ocean and put ourselves right in the path of the bomb. They won't dare do it then.

GRANNY: I want a corner piece.

JANET: Good. That's the most pleasant thing anyone has said to me all day.

JANET starts cutting the cake.

LILY: Did you hear me, Mum?

JANET: I am trying very hard not to hear you.

LILY: We're meeting at 7:00. I'm going as soon as we're done.

JANET: You are not going anywhere, young lady. We are having a nice family get-together.

LILY: A nice family get-together? We haven't had a nice family get-together in about ten years!! Open your eyes, Mum! Do you think Dad is really having a MEETING with his secretary??! Have you seen her?????

Deathly pause.

I am just saying that I'm going to this protest whether you like it or not... This looks yummy. Is it the banana chocolate?

GRANNY: Open that gift! I want to see what I gave you.

LILY opens the box and looks in. She takes out a silver tea service.

I gave you my silver tea service?

JANET: We talked about this, Mum. You wanted to give something nice to Lily.

GRANNY: My good friend Eleanor gave me that tea service for my wedding present. I promised it to Amy.

JANET: Well, now you've given it to Lily for her seventeenth birthday. Isn't that nice.

LILY: I don't even want the stupid tea service! You two are making me mental. The whole world is falling apart and you think I want a silver tea pot? What the fuck am going to do with that???

JANET: Language!!!

LILY: What do you think they want to test that bomb for? Ms. Cluninger says they could use it in Vietnam. Where Robbie is.

JANET: Robbie is serving his country.

LILY: Oh my god! Do you ever hear yourself?

LILY gets ready to leave.

JANET: You will go to that protest over my dead body.

LILY: Well, then hand me the gun, because I'm outta here.

JANET: You haven't even had cake!!!

LILY jams a piece of cake in her mouth.

You had better be home by nine or I'll….!

LILY: All right, I'll be home by nine, happy now??

JANET: Don't speak with your mouth full!!

LILY is gone. We hear the slamming of the front door. It echoes throughout the house. JANET sits down in a chair, on the verge of tears. After a moment:

GRANNY: Your father was a bastard, too.

JANET: Please, Mother…

GRANNY: Do you love him?

JANET: He's my husband. Of course I love him…At least he doesn't lay a hand on me. I'll take Jim over Craig any day.

Pause.

GRANNY: Were you worried I would think you were slutty? I could have arranged something for you. Not a back alley. But a doctor the nurse told me about. But then I guess we wouldn't have that girl yelling at us and stomping around in her rubby get-up.

JANET: I do not want to talk about this.

JANET puts the presents away.

GRANNY: Was I that awful that you couldn't talk to me?

JANET: You certainly weren't very nice.

GRANNY: Amy was so easy to love. She always looked pretty: her hair the latest style. Valedictorian. Class president. Graduated with honours. Made me proud.

JANET: Yes, I know. Amy was better at everything.

GRANNY: You…were difficult.

JANET serves up some cake for GRANNY.

JANET: A corner piece. There you go…

JANET sighs.

Would you like an extra Smartie?

GRANNY touches JANET's arm, startling her.

GRANNY: I wanted to stop you, but…your father wouldn't let me. All the presents had been bought. The toasters and the china with dogwoods on the rim. The Wiggins had given you the crystal wine set.

JANET: My dress. His suit.

JANET stares at the cake.

GRANNY: Think I'll put my feet up in front of the booby tube. My bunions are giving me the gears.

GRANNY fiddles with her cane, gets up stiffly to leave.

JANET: Mum?

GRANNY: Mmm?

JANET: Would you like a hot-water bottle for your feet?

GRANNY: That'd be nice, dear.

JANET: I'll hot the water up in a bit and then I'll bring your cake in to you.

GRANNY goes up to the TV. JANET finds a red Smartie and puts it on GRANNY's cake. We hear the TV go on. It's The Lawrence Welk Show. *JANET pours herself some sherry. She sips the sherry, then makes a decision and goes to the phone. She picks it up and dials.*

Oh…hello? I'm calling for Jim Wilson… It's his wife, Mrs. Wilson…are you his new secretary? …oh…I see…they've gone out… both of them? …I thought…

JANET hangs up the phone. She notices the balloon. She unties it from the chair and hugs it to her chest until it pops. Then she sits down at the table, pulls the cake towards her and is about to dig in when…the Moon Music sneaks in. The MOONWALKER enters. Janet turns and sees him and the music becomes sweeping ballroom dance music. The MOONWALKER offers his hand and they dance together for a bit, enjoying the floating feeling of the music. The MOONWALKER starts to float away and JANET grabs him by his glove before he can float too far. JANET holds him for a while, pleased with herself, before his glove comes off in her hand and he drifts away.

17. What a World, What a World

GRANNY is watching TV. JANET is in her slip, housecoat, and slippers, hair slightly dishevelled: madly making red tissue paper flowers. The skin on her hands and up to her elbows is covered in red dye. She pours a glug-glug of sherry in her tea cup as well as a couple of GRANNY's pills. She gives it all a stir and takes a long sip before returning to the flowers. LILY enters, home from school.

LILY: You won't believe how much stupid homework I have. I don't even know why I go to school in the first place. They just want to turn out little consumers to perpetuate their –

She looks at her mother.

Why are you in your housecoat?

Pause.

Mum? Are you okay?

Pause.

The cake was really good, I scarfed about three pieces when I got back last night.

JANET: Oh…and what time was that?

LILY: Not too late.

JANET: Because I was awake at ten and you certainly were not home.

LILY: Must have been just after that.

JANET: Don't try to pull the wool over me, I was still up at midnight, waiting for your f –... frantic with worry, imagining you in a ditch somewhere or trampled by all those marchers. I had one hand on the phone ready to call the police, when I heard you waltz in. La-di-dah, no care for anyone but yourself.

LILY: Mum. It was such a gas. We marched down Granville Street, holding candles and singing songs. All the way to the American Consulate. And then some official people came and talked to us. There must have been about 10,000 people there! And then Ms. Cluninger had me back to her house and we just talked. About everything. Women's rights. Black people's rights. The Pill. Pollution. Pesticides. The war in Vietnam. Did you know they are killing rice farmers and babies there? That they've been lying about the body counts and that something like 40,000 soldiers have been killed, about one quarter under the age of twenty?

JANET: I am *trying* to get these flowers finished. It happens to be that in very short order Her Majesty will arrive and your mother is now in charge of making all the flowers. All of them. Because too-big-for-her-britches Sheila Witherspoon has turned everyone in the IODE against me. Suddenly they don't like the idea of making these flowers, after we had a meeting three months ago that approved the making of the flowers and today I find out I am the only one who seems to care that we made a commitment, and in less than forty-eight hours that airplane is going to land and Our Queen, Prince Philip, and Princess Anne are going to step out onto the tarmac and see that I've gained seven pounds from all the worrying and I'm going to have to wear those ghastly support hose, because my varicose veins –

LILY: Mum! Don't get so uptight. I'll help you.

JANET: *(Sarcastic.)* Ooooh, that would be nice. If you can take time from your busy schedule with your precious Mrs. Cluninger.

LILY: Mum, she's so cool, you'd really like her. She's making me see the world in a whole new way.

JANET: Well, I can see that it's not her place to be putting wild ideas in students' heads. She should stick to teaching Home Economics.

(JANET rises.) I'm of a mind to call up the principal and give him what-for… *(She goes to the phone.)* That woman teaching you all this women's lib hoohah.

LILY: Mum! Don't you dare! I'd never ever, ever, ever, ever, ever forgive you.

JANET: From now on, you stay away from her –

LILY: No!

JANET: You heard me.

LILY: *She'd never* be at the mercy of a man. Waiting around all night for him to come home so she can be his maid. Like you are for Dad, some kind of servant-wife-slave. Can't you see he's treating you like shit?

JANET: Don't speak ill of your father. He is a good man. A good provider. He is my husband!!

JANET continues to make the flowers, with determination.

LILY: I saw them, you know. Dad and his "secretary" Ivanka in that French restaurant on Robson. We were just leaving and singing songs, walking back to the bus stop and all of a sudden my head turned, like it was being pulled by a string. Dad and that Ivanka woman right in the front window, holding hands. All kissy-kissy. I just about barfed. That's why I went to Ms. Cluninger's house, because I didn't know what to say to you. But you really need to face it, Mum. Your husband is a bastard.

Mum, did you hear me? You need to get heavy with him. Lay it down. Tell him that you won't take his kind of bullshit anymore!

JANET: Can you not see I'm busy here?

LILY: Right. Making stupid paper flowers to impress some symbol of colonialism. Why don't you take another pill while you're at it? Wash it down with a bunch of booze… I hate it here.

LILY grabs her books and goes into the rec room and lies on the couch. JANET catches her breath, adds some sherry to her tea, and takes another big swig. After a moment, as if the wind is gently blowing him in, ROBBIE enters. He is now twenty-one. His hair is neatly cropped and he wears his army uniform.

ROBBIE: What a trip… Is this for real?

JANET: Robbie! You're back! Come in, come in! Careful of the flowers.

ROBBIE: What's with the wild garden of red, Aunty J?

JANET: They are for a very special day, Robbie. Her Majesty Queen Elizabeth is coming to celebrate our centenary. And your Aunty Janet has been asked to be part of the welcoming committee, greet her at the airport. Give her a fresh bouquet of spring blossoms. I'm also responsible for making some paper flowers to decorate the handrails, make things festive and welcoming. They're peonies, can you tell?

ROBBIE: You've been chosen to meet the Number One Lady? Far out!

JANET: Thank you, Robbie, you're the first one of our family to show some enthusiasm. It's really an honour. Protocol sent me quite the list of dos and don'ts. Tips for executing a proper curtsy –

JANET attempts a deep, proper curtsy, but sways under the influence of the pills and booze.

– you can't speak to her unless she speaks to you first –

ROBBIE: Well she's the Queen-Bee, right? You can't be just be jammin' and whamming, you gotta show some –

JANET: Everyone wants a piece of her. She has to travel with her own toilet seat! Otherwise people will steal them, as a souvenir. Can you imagine?

ROBBIE: That blows my mind!

JANET: But here I am chatting away, silly as a lark bird, when you've just got back! Did you make some nice friends over there? I remember the men who went over to W-W Two saying that they had such a sense of camaraderie. How did it all go?

ROBBIE: Day one they put me in a chopper and plunked me in the jungle. Soon as my boots touched the old terra firma, the whole world went kazoom. Buddy I had been blowing Double-Bubbles with five minutes earlier explodes into gobs of blood: bones popping through his skin, intestines pouring out of his stomach. Deader than Jesus. Everything outta control loud... bombs, screams, heartbeat so crazy my ears stopped working. Charlie shooting at me, but couldn't see where from so I just blasted everything that twitched with my M-16: old peasant ladies, pregnant women, kids, dogs. First day.

I became so good at exploding stuff. A fucking expert. I betcha I blew up like... I loved the way things lit up the sky because it meant I was still living. My skin soaked up the smell of death till it made me feel itchy. Even rations tasted like death. But if I could see something beautiful – then my heart was beat-a-beating.

Day I left...Tromping through the jungle with the old section. Ragtag bunch. Sweat dripping. Boots scrunching in mud. Wild shades of tangled greens; trees, moss, ferns, grass, bamboo. Birds with their crazy whistling. I eye this plant. Bloom the size of my fist, scarlet, like a gaping mouth with the tongue sticking out. Blah!! The botanist dude from Texas says it's a ginger lily. And I go for it, thinking I'll put that bud on my helmet – pirate style – and wham.

JANET: Wham?

ROBBIE: You get my drift? Kool-Aid. Clusterfuck.

GRANNY appears, tottering with her cane.

GRANNY: Lord love a duck. Who are you talking to, Janet?

ROBBIE has gone, having slipped out on the same breeze that brought him in. JANET stares, unable to speak.

Why haven't you started dinner? I'm starving.

GRANNY notices JANET's fragile state.

What the bejesus is wrong with you? You look like you've lost your marbles.

JANET's mouth moves like a fish's, no sound emerging.

I'm going to call Jim and tell that asshole to get home and take control of this house.

Transitional Music, suggested style: Country Joe McDonald, "I-Feel-Like-I'm-Fixin'-To-Die Rag."

18. Kool-Aid

JANET has prepared breakfast. A vase of turquoise blue carnations sits on the counter. The tissue-paper flowers have all been piled into mounds of wicker baskets, set and ready to go. Janet has a happy spring to her step as she lays out several pairs of gloves over the back of a chair.

JANET: *(To herself, by rote.)* Elizabeth the second, George the sixth, Edward the eighth, George the fifth, Edward the seventh. Victoria, William the fourth, George the fourth, George the third…

GRANNY enters slowly, teetering on her cane, finding her seat at the breakfast table. JANET gets GRANNY's breakfast plate and puts it on the table. GRANNY stares at it for a moment, pokes it.

GRANNY: What's this?

JANET: It's toad-in-a-hole, Mum. Just like you asked.

JANET mixes up some Tang as she calls:

Lily, breakfast!

GRANNY: *(Suspicious.)* Hmmmmm.

JANET: What's wrong with it?

GRANNY: I don't remember toad-in-a-hole looking like that.

JANET: *(Still cheery.)* Cut a hole in buttered bread, crack an egg in it. Fry. Both sides. That's what it is. Like it or lump it.

LILY drags her sleepy, dishevelled body in and sits at the table.

Good-morning, Lilibet Wilson. Toad-in-a-hole?

JANET puts another plate in front of LILY.

LILY: That looks revolting.

JANET: Like it or lump it, Grumplepumps. The sun is shining, the forecast is good, and your mother is about to go address four patrols of Girl Guides and a pack of Brownies who are helping attach the flowers to the railings. Then I am dropping into the florist to check the progress on the bouquet that I am presenting to Her Majesty tomorrow. Tomorrow! Tomorrow! Pinch me! Remember, we will be leaving at 10:00 a.m. sharp. Your father's giving up his Shriners' duties for the day. I'd like to give your hair a trim tonight, Lily. Neaten it up a bit. Mother, I've taken your wool dress out of the mothballs to air it out. Might be chilly on the tarmac. I've checked the arrangements, and you'll have to wait some twenty feet back, but if we get there early enough you should still have a good view. Lily, I'm going to put you on photo duty. You'll want to practise using the camera wearing gloves. I've put out a few pairs for you both to try on and –

LILY: I'm not wearing gloves. I haven't worn gloves since I went to church and that was about a million years ago.

GRANNY: This egg is as hard as rubber. You know I like them coddled.

JANET: Perhaps you naysayers would like to glance up and notice the pretty flowers on the counter.

GRANNY: What the hell are those?

JANET: Jim gave me those carnations. With a lovely Hallmark card.

GRANNY: Carnations aren't blue like that. Those are unnatural. This house is unnatural.

LILY: What? He thinks a bunch of flowers is going to make it all better? You're joking.

JANET: And! A box of Laura Secord assorted creams.

LILY: Oh, well then.

JANET: Nothing you do or say is going to get me down today. I've been looking forward to –

The phone rings. Very loudly.

Oh, my goodness, I bet that's Sheila Witherspoon. Apparently she's eaten crow and wants to get in on all the celebrations. Try to take credit for how it's all coming off so nicely –

JANET answers the phone.

Wilson residence... *(Loudly.)* Oh hi, Amy! You've just caught us right in the middle of our preparations for the big day tomorrow. Lily's going to wear your confirmation gloves –

GRANNY: Amy?

JANET: What did you say?... I can't understand you. Calm down now...take a breath, Amy... Has...*(Low.)* Craig done something......? What about Robbie?... He's...what?

She listens for a moment.

LILY: Mum?

JANET looks at LILY and drops the phone. It dangles by the cord. Red petals drift down from the sky.

Transitional music. Stylistic choices: Joni Mitchell's "Woodstock," "River," or "Circle Game." Or perhaps Scott McKenzie's "San Francisco (Be Sure to Wear Some Flowers In Your Hair)."

Janet (Marion Day) tries to absorb tragic news as Lily (Katie Ryerson) and Granny (Beverley Wolfe) attempt to understand the significance of the moment.

Photo by Martin Conboy.

19. I Can't Change, I Won't Change

JANET is alone on stage. She wears a nice coat, a hat, and gloves and carries some fresh flowers.

JANET: It was a little blustery but otherwise a perfectly beautiful day. We arrived an hour ahead just liked they asked. I presented myself to the fellow from protocol and he went over the rules, but he needn't have for my sake. I was prepared. Acknowledge royalty with a small curtsy. Only shake the Queen's hand if she offers it to you first. Do not begin a conversation with the Queen; wait till she begins talking to you. She is to be addressed as "Your Majesty the Queen" and he is "Your Royal Highness."

The crowd was enormous, hundreds of people… I could see Jim, Lily, and Mum staked at their spots behind the railings that were covered in the tissue flowers. They looked spectacular, if I do say so. Brownies did a nice job of attaching them, with my supervision, of course. An ocean wave of red and white peonies.

I wasn't part of the crowd, I was separated, right on the tarmac at the end of the red carpet with two others who had been chosen: a little polio girl and a Korean War Veteran. My bouquet of spring mix looked terrific. Tammy from the IODE had connections with a florist and they went all out.

The airplane came into sight and landed without a hitch, coming to rest right at the carpet, the stairs quickly put in place. And then there she was. Alighting the plane. Looking wonderful. All in red, for us, for

Canada: a smart scarlet coat and a matching hat with large white flowers, rather in the shape of a mushroom cap. Very clever, really – set firmly on her head. She came down onto the carpet, Philip a gentle distance behind, followed by Anne. She's quite stately, Anne. The dignitaries were lined up; Mr. Trudeau and his new, young wife, Margaret Sinclair, wearing a big floppy hat; Governor General Roland Michener was there with his better half.

Then…Her Majesty walked towards us three special people. She took the small posy from the polio girl, nodded seriously to the soldier as he told her some tale or other, and then it was my turn. My turn.

I could feel her presence moving towards me. I placed my right foot behind my left heel, my knees just starting to bend, in a perfect graceful curtsy. The queen's blue-grey eyes were scanning where to rest, her right hand preparing to take the flowers from my arms, I let myself smile just a little, she must have been but a foot away from me and then… It was right at that very moment that… something caught the Queen's attention: Maggie Trudeau lost control of her big floppy hat, it was blowing down the tarmac and an RCMP officer was running after it. The Queen stopped. She turned. Away from me. She saw the commotion surrounding the floppy hat. She moved toward the action, she passed me by. The Queen of England went over to Maggie Trudeau, shared a laugh with her about the silly hat. And she didn't return for my bouquet.

Janet (Marion Day) speaks about the day the Queen came to town.
Photo by Martin Conboy.

Protocol did not speak up to tell her she had made a mistake. Anne did not place her hand on her mother's elbow to steer her back to duty. Philip was too busy sharing a chuckle with Mr. Michener to notice me. Nobody noticed me. That was my moment and it was missed. All because of that fuddle-duddling Maggie Trudeau: the pretty young wife with her whole life ahead of her, her whole happy life ahead of her. That was the closest I came to royalty. One foot away.

Transitional music: suggested style "Morning Has Broken" by Cat Stevens.

20. This Is the End

There are piles of laundry and the ironing board is set up. JANET stands at the window looking outside at the rain. She has her apron on. GRANNY is sound asleep, hunched over the kitchen table, in an odd position. LILY comes in. She watches her mother for a moment.

LILY: Mum.

Pause.

There's something I want to talk to you about.

JANET: Hmmm?

LILY: Ms. Cluninger's going to Stanford University. To get a master's degree. Did you know that Stanford has a student advocacy group that fights for the civil rights of…everyone? It's so cool. I'm thinking of moving there, too. I could help Aunt Amy. Keep her company. Get involved in the anti-war stuff. Do something with my life instead of rotting here.

Pause.

Did you hear what I said, Mum?

JANET: San Francisco.

LILY: Ms. Cluninger has had it with Home Economics. All she gets is complaints from parents who want their daughters to learn how to make the perfect soufflé. It's so crazy.

JANET: Maybe I'll make a soufflé for supper. I've got some Emmental cheese that would be nice in it.

LILY: I'm sure it's okay with Dad. He doesn't care what I do.

JANET: Well if your father thinks it's all right…

LILY: Okay then.

JANET is still looking out the window. LILY comes behind her and gives her mum a hug. Then LILY leaves the room. After a moment.

JANET: *(To her audience.)* Tea anyone? I thought I'd make a pot of Earl Grey.

The End.

Transitional music takes us out: suggested style: John Maus' "Hey Moon."